Quiet Hour

Quiet Hour

An Easy Way to Reduce Stress
and Feel Inner Peace Outside

Heather Chase and Ken Beller

LTS Press

Published by LTS Press, P.O. Box 4165, Sedona, AZ 86336, info@LTSPress.com

ISBN 978-0-9801382-6-9 (softcover)
ISBN 978-0-9801382-1-4 (ebook)

This book may be purchased in bulk for promotional, educational, or business use. Please contact the publisher at the above address or email for information or to order.

Cover photos and photo 1: Heather Chase; photo 2: Unsplash.com, Inspa Makers; photo 3: iStockphoto.com, Michael H; photo 4: Unsplash.com, Brock; photo 5: 123RF.com, Ivan Kimt; photo 6: Unsplash.com, Jasmin Chew; photo 7: Unsplash.com, Christian Wiediger; photo 8: NPS; photo 9: 123RF.com, soloway.

CONTENTS

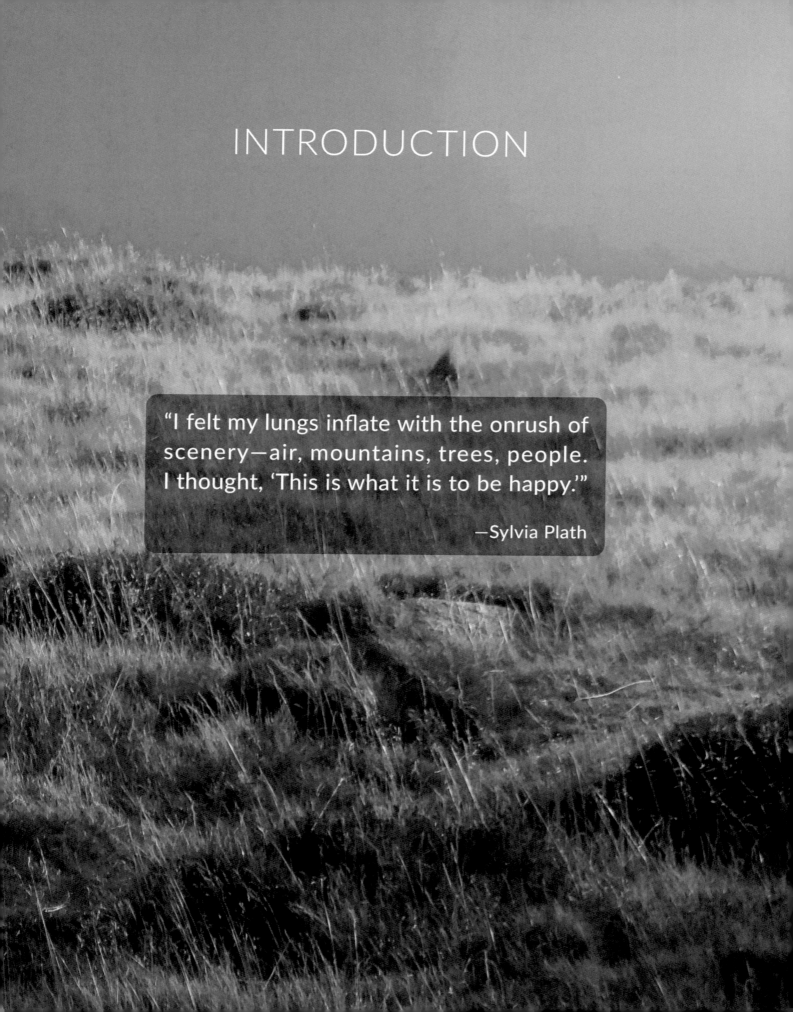

INTRODUCTION

"I felt my lungs inflate with the onrush of scenery—air, mountains, trees, people. I thought, 'This is what it is to be happy.'"

—Sylvia Plath

TODAY'S NOISE AND STRESS PROBLEM

Rumbling traffic... blaring car alarms... pinging message alerts... upsetting 24-hour news—today we are more bombarded with noise and stress than ever in human history. We might try to ignore them or get used to them, but they take a bigger toll on us than we realize.

They are such a problem that the World Health Organization considers noise from traffic one of the worst environmental stressors for humans and calls stress the health epidemic of the twenty-first century.

Chronic noise causes stress, which in turn causes health problems. As *The Nature Fix* author Florence Williams points out, "Noise may well be the most pervasive pollutant in America."

In fact, as published in the *American Journal of Industrial Medicine*, the *American Journal of Preventive Medicine*, and other sources, research shows that health risks of chronic noise exposure may include:

- Increased stress hormones
- Sleep disturbance
- Hearing impairment and tinnitus
- Triggers for people with post-traumatic stress disorder
- Changes in the immune system
- Hypertension and ischemic heart disease
- Diabetes
- Aggression, violence, and other anti-social behaviors
- Anxiety, depression, and other psychiatric disorders
- Birth defects
- Early death (In the E.U., noise is considered a factor in ~10,000 deaths per year.)

AN APPEALING SOLUTION

To reduce the impact of noise and stress, we might be tempted to hide out and wear ear plugs all the time. But there is a more appealing solution: quiet breaks in natural settings. Research study after study shows exposure to quiet and nature reduces stress.

In fact, this has been confirmed in well over a hundred studies. Plus, research indicates nature can meet psychological and emotional needs that are difficult to meet any other way.

For example, research shows people who spend at least two hours in nature each week report significantly better health and well-being.

Publications by the American Heart Association, the American Psychological Association, and other sources reveal that some benefits of time in nature may include:

- Reduced stress/mental distress

- Decreased anxiety and depression

- Better mood/happiness

- Increased energy

- Improved heart health

- Increased positive social interactions

- Better self-esteem and concentration

- Increased memory, creativity, and work satisfaction

- Increased sense of belonging, meaning, and purpose in life

- Living longer

But in today's noisy, hectic, high-tech world, these benefits often seem out of reach since we are more cut off from quiet and nature than ever.

So, stress is a chronic, widespread problem and quiet time in the outdoors can help solve it. But most of us don't know how powerful this solution is, how to get the recommended two hours a week, or how to make the most of time in nature to reduce our stress.

Quiet Hour can help.

WHAT IS QUIET HOUR?

The ready-to-do, step-by-step Quiet Hour process makes getting the benefits of quiet and nature easy! This soothing process helps you, or people you lead or serve, enjoy the stress-relief benefits of being quietly present in natural settings. It is an easy way to de-stress, relax, and connect with nature.

The process is done seated and is for people of all physical ability levels. It incorporates several techniques that research indicates have a calming or uplifting effect. It smoothly blends these techniques into, basically, a simple 4-step process. Those steps include:

- Gather
- Breathe
- Notice
- Appreciate

Woven into that 4-step process, the calming or uplifting techniques explored include:

- Exposure to nature
- Quiet
- Pausing electronic device use
- Earthing/grounding
- Extended exhale breathing
- Sensory awareness
- Effortless attention/soft fascination
- Opportunities for awe
- Gratitude

For added convenience, the program can be done for a full hour, or a half hour, and this book offers step-by-step guidance for both options.

BENEFITS FOR INDIVIDUALS

If you want to do Quiet Hour by yourself, it can help you in many ways. The program is:

- A new way to reduce stress. It turns your yard, a nearby park, or any natural spot into a sanctuary where you can relax, replenish, and savor being alive on our beautiful planet.

- A new way to experience nature—not by learning about it, playing in it, or exercising in it, but by feeling inner peace in it. While you might have felt this by chance on your own, Quiet Hour is a structured, guided way to feel it often.

- Easy to do. The soothing process can be done while sitting or lying down. Its pace is relaxed, and the portable guidance summary cards make it easy to do in any natural spot.

- Flexible. The timing is adjustable. For example, if you're short on time, or have children younger than age 12 and would like to include them, you can shorten each step of the program and make it Quiet Half-Hour or even Quiet Quarter-Hour for a quick break.

BENEFITS FOR GROUP LEADERS

If you serve groups of people, such as public land visitors, school classes, youth groups, and so on, Quiet Hour can also help you in many ways. The program is:

- A new way to serve participants and your community, turning local natural spaces into a stress-relief and wellness resource.

- Likely to increase participants' emotional connection with your organization, and their emotional connection with, and desire to protect, nature—their conservation ethic.

- A way to measure impact. Optional surveys allow you to instantly collect feedback from participants and other leaders to access the program's effectiveness.

- Flexible. The timing is adjustable. For example, for a version for children under age 12, each step of the process can be shortened, and the name changed to Quiet Half-Hour.

- Easy to incorporate. It is easy to add to a current collection of staff- or volunteer-led programs or as a stand-alone program. To conduct it, you do not need any special training and can simply follow the steps in the "For Group Leaders" section. That section has practically everything you need to lead Quiet Hour regularly or test it in a pilot program. Suggestions in it can be adjusted for your organization's specific needs or for specific audiences.

- Easy to conduct. It involves little speaking, very few materials, and no expertise, physical fitness, or equipment. The relaxed pace gives you time to preview each step of narration as you go and for narration to be bilingual or interpreted into sign language, if needed.

Whether you do Quiet Hour alone or with a group, the authors hope you enjoy it, practice it often, and that it becomes a positive part of your life. Further, through you, they hope it helps create a positive ripple effect out into society.

FOR INDIVIDUALS

"For a time I rest in the grace of the world, and am free."

—Wendell Berry

GUIDANCE FOR INDIVIDUALS

Below are three versions of the Quiet Hour process—a full version, a simple one-page summary, and even simpler summary cards. Your first few times doing Quiet Hour, it's best to use the full version. Once you are familiar with it, or want to do Quiet Half-Hour, you might switch to one of the summaries to use often outdoors.

Also, if it is more comfortable for you, you might read the full guidance, but do it as a half-hour version a few times first and then move up to the full hour version.

What You'll Need

- 1 Hour (1/2 hr. if doing Quiet Half-Hour as on Summary and Summary Cards)

- 1 Watch or clock

- 1 Copy of Full Guidance, Guidance for Individuals Summary, or Guidance for Individuals Summary Card

- Anything else you might need for your safety or comfort, such as insect repellent, etc.

FULL GUIDANCE

1. Agreements, 0 min.

To get the benefits of this program, it helps to follow two agreements.

Agreement 1 is to detach from devices. It's best to turn off your phone, smart watch, camera, etc., or put your phone in airplane mode, and put them away in your pocket or bag. Try not to use devices unless something is urgent. If you want to take pictures, it's best to wait until after the program.

Agreement 2 is to maintain quiet. If you are doing this with someone else, it's best to agree not to talk unless something is urgent.

Other than those two things, everything else is optional. This is your experience. If you don't feel like doing a step, that's completely fine.

2. Get Comfortable, 5 min.

Find a natural spot outside and get comfortable. You can sit on the ground, lean against a tree, or even lie down.

If you like, you can take your shoes off and put your feet on the ground. From now on, feel free to change position to stay comfortable. Settle in and relax any tension in your body.

3. Main 4-Step Process

Step 1: Gather, 5 min.

You're invited to gather your thoughts and energy from all the different directions they've been in. Let everything else pause, knowing it will still be there after this experience. Bring your attention to right here, right now. Let yourself have the gift of this time.

Step 2: Breathe, 5 min.

You might become aware of your breathing. Inhale, feeling your chest expand, and exhale, feeling it contract. You might gently extend your exhale—like inhale 1, 2, 3, exhale 1, 2, 3, 4; or inhale 1, 2, 3, exhale 1, 2, 3, 4, 5. Breathe that way for a few minutes.

Step 3: Notice

Notice—Feeling, 5 min.

Maybe notice what your body is feeling. Where is it touching something? Feel what you're sitting, standing, or lying on supporting you. How does the sunlight feel? How about the air?

Notice—Seeing, 5 min.

Notice what you're seeing. What colors and objects are here? What's at eye level, above, and below? What do you see nearby? How about further away?

Notice—Hearing, 5 min.

You might notice what you're hearing. What sounds are here? What are the main sounds and the quieter ones? What do you hear nearby? How about further away?

Notice—Smelling, 5 min.

Notice what you're smelling. Does this place have an overall aroma? How about some individual things here? Feel free to find some natural things near you, like plants or rocks, and smell them.

Notice—It All, 20 min.

You're welcome to relax your focus and notice it all together, the whole natural system here. Let your awareness open and expand. Relax and just be.

Step 4: Appreciate, 5 min.

If you like, feel grateful for something here. Did you especially like something, maybe the fresh air or the warm sunshine? You might appreciate it all, everything that added to your experience. Lastly, maybe appreciate yourself for taking time to do this process. Feel free to give a gesture of appreciation, like a nod, if you like.

HANDLING POTENTIAL CHALLENGES

The following is not part of the main process unless needed. If the following challenges arise, handle them using your best judgment or these suggestions.

Human-Made Background Noise

It helps to realize that often stress comes from resisting what is. To reduce that stress, we can relax our resistance to the sound, let it be what it is, and shift our focus to more pleasant sounds. Also, humans are part of nature, too, and we can let their sounds blend with the other sounds.

Unpleasant Weather

Again, it helps to realize that often stress comes from resisting what is. To reduce that stress, we can relax our resistance to the weather, let it be what it is, and shift our focus to something positive about it. For example, wind can be uncomfortable but also refreshing.

Restlessness

Take a short break. Maybe stretch a bit. If you like, turn and face a different direction. Do the extended exhale breathing for a few more breaths. It might also help to imagine you're a toddler, experiencing a place like this for the first time, with wonder and delight. Then continue from where you were before the break. If needed, shorten the Notice—It All step.

HELPFUL HINTS

Choosing Spots and Times

Quiet Hour can be done in many spots, such as a local park, nature center, or your own yard. Online tools for finding spots near you are in the "Resources" section. In choosing spots, you might favor ones with features such as quiet areas away from busy roads; water sources such as ponds, birdbaths, or fountains; and native plants and trees that attract wildlife.

You can do Quiet Hour anytime, such as during your lunch break or on your day off. Some especially enjoyable times can be sunrise and sunset with their beautiful colors and different seasons with their various weather conditions.

Most importantly, do Quiet Hour when and where it is convenient for you, so you will do it often and enjoy the benefits long-term.

Practicing with Others

After enjoying Quiet Hour by yourself or with another person, you might like to invite more friends, relatives, or colleagues to practice it with you. For example, you could lead a group of your coworkers in doing Quiet Hour regularly, once a week. To make practicing with others easy, use the guidance in the "For Group Leaders" section.

QUIET HOUR
GUIDANCE FOR INDIVIDUALS SUMMARY

Once you are somewhat familiar with the Quiet Hour process, you might like to print or photocopy this summary, then use its reminders of the concepts in the full version.

Step	~Minutes for 1 hr.	~Running Total
Agreements Detach from devices, maintain quiet	0	0
Get Comfortable Find natural spot, maybe take off shoes	5	5
Gather Bring your thoughts and energy to here and now	5	10
Breathe Maybe extend exhale, in 1, 2, 3, out 1, 2, 3, 4	5	15
Notice—Feeling The surface supporting you, sunlight, air	5	20
Notice—Seeing At eye-level, above, below, near, far	5	25
Notice—Hearing Main sounds, quieter sounds, near, far	5	30
Notice—Smelling Overall scent, individual natural things	5	35
Notice—It All For a longer time, relax, just be	20	55
Appreciate Something here, it all, yourself for doing this	5	60

Handling Potential Challenges

Human-Made Noise Relax resistance, shift focus, humans are part of nature too

Weather Relax resistance, shift focus to something positive about it

Restlessness Stretch, face different direction, extended exhale breathing, resume

QuietHour.org

QUIET HALF-HOUR
GUIDANCE FOR INDIVIDUALS SUMMARY

Once you are somewhat familiar with the Quiet Hour process, you might like to print or photocopy this summary, then use its reminders of the concepts in the full version.

Step	~Minutes for 1/2 hr.	~Running Total
Agreements Detach from devices, maintain quiet	0	0
Get Comfortable Find natural spot, maybe take off shoes	3	3
Gather Bring your thoughts and energy to here and now	3	6
Breathe Maybe extend exhale, in 1, 2, 3, out 1, 2, 3, 4	3	9
Notice—Feeling The surface supporting you, sunlight, air	3	12
Notice—Seeing At eye-level, above, below, near, far	3	15
Notice—Hearing Main sounds, quieter sounds, near, far	3	18
Notice—Smelling Overall scent, individual natural things	3	21
Notice—It All For a longer time, relax, just be	6	27
Appreciate Something here, it all, yourself for doing this	3	30

Handling Potential Challenges

Human-Made Noise Relax resistance, shift focus, humans are part of nature too

Weather Relax resistance, shift focus to something positive about it

Restlessness Stretch, face different direction, extended exhale breathing, resume

QuietHour.org

GUIDANCE FOR INDIVIDUALS SUMMARY CARDS

Once you are very familiar with the Quiet Hour process, you're welcome to use the following convenient, pocket-sized summary cards. Just print or photocopy this page, cut out the cards, and laminate them to use often. One is for an hour-long session and the other is for a half-hour session.

QUIET HOUR GUIDANCE

Step	~Minutes for 1 hr.	~Running Total
Agreements	0	0
Get Comfortable	5	5
Gather	5	10
Breathe	5	15
Notice—Feeling	5	20
Notice—Seeing	5	25
Notice—Hearing	5	30
Notice—Smelling	5	35
Notice—It All	20	55
Appreciate	5	60

QuietHour.org

QUIET HALF-HOUR GUIDANCE

Step	~Minutes for 30 min.	~Running Total
Agreements	0	0
Get Comfortable	3	3
Gather	3	6
Breathe	3	9
Notice—Feeling	3	12
Notice—Seeing	3	15
Notice—Hearing	3	18
Notice—Smelling	3	21
Notice—It All	6	27
Appreciate	3	30

QuietHour.org

EXPERIENCE LOG

If you like, use the following log to reflect on your Quiet Hour sessions. Feel free to photocopy it to use for many sessions. Fill in when and where you did each session and how you felt the experience went, how you felt after it, etc.

Date	Location	Experience

FOR GROUP LEADERS

"One touch of nature makes the whole world kin."

—William Shakespeare

GUIDANCE FOR GROUP LEADERS

Timing and Materials

- 1 Hour (more if doing survey and offering gift, less if shortening to Quiet Half-Hour)

- 1 Watch or clock for the leader

- 1 Full Narration or Guidance for Group Leaders Summary for the leader

- (Optional) 1 Participant Survey Card and pen for each participant

- (Optional) 1 Participant Gift (a copy of the Guidance for Individuals Summary Card) for each participant to take with them at the end of the session

- Anything else that might be needed for participants' safety or comfort

Introduction to Narration

Create a safe, positive experience using the following sample guidance narration. Words in *[CAPITALS, BRACKETS, AND ITALICS]* are notes to you or words for you to fill in.

You may read each part silently before starting and during the long pauses in the process. Then say each part as written or in your own words.

FULL GUIDANCE

Below are two versions of the narration—a full word-for-word version, and a shorter one-page summary. Your first few times leading the program, it's best to use the full version. Once you are familiar with it, you might switch to the shorter version for easier use on-site.

1. *[INTRODUCTION, 4 MIN.]*

Welcome. *[IF AVAILABLE, ASK, OR HAVE AN INTERPRETER ASK, IN A SECOND LANGUAGE, "WELCOME. DOES ANYONE NEED INTERPRETATION IN THIS LANGUAGE?" IF SO, MAKE TIME FOR IT AND, IF NEEDED, SHORTEN THE NOTICE—IT ALL STEP.]*

Thank you for being here today. I'm *[NAME, TITLE]*. Today we're in for a treat. We'll get a rare break from noise and busy-ness and have a chance to de-stress, relax, and connect with nature in a new way.

We'll do this through a peaceful process. It's a blend of techniques that research indicates can help relax our bodies, calm our minds, and improve our mood. Sound good?

2. *[AGREEMENTS, 4 MIN.]*

To get those benefits, and let everyone else get them, it helps if we can follow two agreements.

Agreement 1 is to detach from devices. We'll turn off our phones, smart watches, cameras, etc., or put our phones in airplane mode. And we'll put them away in our pockets or bags. We won't use devices unless something is urgent. In that case, we'll step away. If we want to take pictures, we'll wait until after the program.

Agreement 2 is to maintain quiet. Other than me guiding you through the process, we won't talk or distract others unless something is urgent. If we have to leave early, we'll leave very quietly.

Other than those two things, everything else is optional. This is your experience. If you don't feel like doing a step, that's completely fine. Please just honor the agreements, as a courtesy to everyone else.

Do you have any questions? [ANSWER AS BEST YOU CAN.]

Okay, do we all agree to the two agreements of detaching from devices and maintaining quiet? [LOOK FOR EVERYONE TO NOD.] Okay, let's silence our devices and put them away. [PAUSE.] And let's start maintaining quiet, except for my guidance.

3. [GET COMFORTABLE, 4 MIN.]

If you like where you are, I invite you to get comfortable. Or you can move to another spot for the rest of the process. You can sit on the ground, lean against a tree, or even lie down. Please find a spot you like, close enough to hear me. [PAUSE.]

It's optional, but if you like, you can take your shoes off and put your feet on the ground, so you're connected to the earth. From now on, feel free to quietly change position to stay comfortable. Can everyone hear me? [LOOK FOR NODS.] Good. Now, please settle in and relax any tension in your body.

4. [MAIN 4-STEP PROCESS (SPEAK SLOWLY. PAUSE ~30 SECONDS BETWEEN SENTENCES.)]

[STEP 1: GATHER, 4 MIN.]

I invite you to gather your thoughts and energy from all the different directions they've been in. Let everything else pause, knowing it will still be there after this experience. Bring your attention to right here, right now. Let yourself have the gift of this time.

[STEP 2: BREATHE, 4 MIN.]

You might become aware of your breathing. Inhale, feel your chest expand and exhale, feel it contract. You might gently extend your exhale, like inhale 1, 2, 3, exhale 1, 2, 3, 4, or inhale 1, 2, 3, exhale 1, 2, 3, 4, 5. Good, you can keep breathing this way on your own.

[STEP 3: NOTICE]

[NOTICE—FEELING, 4 MIN.]

I invite you to notice what your body is feeling. Where is it touching something? Feel what you're sitting, standing, or lying on supporting you. How does the sunlight feel? How about the air?

[NOTICE—SEEING, 4 MIN.]

Feel free to notice what you're seeing. What colors and objects are here? What's at eye-level, above, and below? What do you see nearby? How about further away?

[NOTICE—HEARING, 4 MIN.]

You might notice what you're hearing. What sounds are here? What are the main sounds and the quieter ones? What do you hear nearby? How about further away?

[NOTICE—SMELLING, 4 MIN.]

I invite you to notice what you're smelling. Does this place have an overall aroma? How about some individual things here? Feel free to find some natural things near you, like plants or rocks, and smell them.

[NOTICE—IT ALL, 10 MIN.]

You might relax your focus and notice it all together, the whole natural system here. Let your awareness open and expand. We'll be in this step longer than the others, about [NUMBER] minutes, and I'll keep track of the time. So, you can relax and just be.

[STEP 4: APPRECIATE, 4 MIN.]

Now you might feel grateful for something here. Did you especially like something here, maybe the fresh air or the warm sunshine? You might appreciate it all, everything that added to your experience. Lastly, maybe appreciate yourself for taking time to do this process. Feel free to do a gesture of appreciation, like a nod, if you like.

5. **[CONCLUSION** (RETURN TO YOUR NORMAL SPEAKING RATE.), 4 MIN.]

As for me, I appreciate you being here today. Thank you for giving this process a try and letting me guide you through it. I hope you enjoyed it.

You can take this process back into your daily life and repeat it at other times, in other places. If you don't have a full hour or a setting like this, you can shorten it to Quiet Half-Hour or Quiet Quarter-Hour... or just do parts of it for a few minutes in any natural spot. You can use it any time, to relax and enjoy nature more fully.

[OPTIONAL] I'd really like to know what you thought of today's program. So, I'd appreciate it if you'd please fill out the short survey on these cards. [SHOW.]

[OPTIONAL] And if you'd like help doing this process on your own, feel free to take one of these summaries of it. [SHOW.]

Thanks again. I hope you have a peaceful rest of your day.

6. **[SURVEY** (OPTIONAL) IF TESTING THIS IN A PILOT PROGRAM, OR COLLECTING FEEDBACK, OFFER PARTICIPANT SURVEY CARDS AND PENS. PAUSE, THEN COLLECT.), 6 MIN.]

7. **[GIFT** (OPTIONAL) IF DESIRED, OFFER THE PARTICIPANT GIFT FOR PARTICIPANTS TO TAKE WITH THEM.]

HANDLING POTENTIAL CHALLENGES

The following is not part of the main narration unless needed. If the following challenges arise, handle them using your best judgment or these suggested responses.

[HUMAN-MADE BACKGROUND NOISE]

Often stress comes from resisting what is. To reduce that stress, we can relax our resistance to the sound, let it be what it is, and shift our focus to more pleasant sounds. Also, humans are part of nature, too, and we can let their sounds blend with the other sounds.

[UNPLEASANT WEATHER]

Often stress comes from resisting what is. To reduce that stress, we can relax our resistance to the weather, let it be what it is, and shift our focus to something positive about it. For example, wind can be uncomfortable but also refreshing.

[RESTLESSNESS]

Let's take a short break. I invite everyone to stretch a bit. *[PAUSE.]* I invite you to turn and face a different direction, while still being able to hear me. *[PAUSE.]* Let's do the extended exhale breathing for a few breaths. *[PAUSE.]* Now, I invite you to imagine you're a toddler, experiencing a place like this for the first time, with wonder and delight. *[PAUSE. THEN RESUME FROM WHERE YOU WERE BEFORE THE BREAK. IF NEEDED, SHORTEN THE STEP CALLED NOTICE—IT ALL.]*

[DISRUPTIVENESS]

[QUIETLY TAKE PARTICIPANT ASIDE. ASK IF THEY NEED ANYTHING. REMIND THEM OF THE AGREEMENTS. IF THEY CONTINUE BEING DISRUPTIVE, FOR THE SAKE OF THE GROUP'S EXPERIENCE, QUIETLY SAY IT SEEMS THIS PROGRAM MIGHT NOT BE A GOOD FIT FOR THEM. ASK IF THEY'D BE HAPPIER LEAVING AND DOING SOMETHING ELSE.]

HELPFUL HINT

Quiet Hour is designed for general audiences. However, to make it relevant to your specific audience, you can add to the introduction. For example, if you're leading a group of students, you might add how quiet time in nature can inspire discovery and creativity, with examples from the lives of people in your discipline. Or, if you're leading a faith-based group, you might add how quiet time in nature can enhance spiritual life, with quotes from books or leaders in your tradition.

PARTICIPANT SURVEY

If you're doing a test or collecting feedback, print or photocopy this page on cardstock as many times as needed, cut out the surveys, and invite participants to complete them at the end of each session.

- -

Did Quiet Hour help you feel less tense or stressed?   Yes   No   Date: _____

Did it help you feel more calm or relaxed?   Yes   No

Would you recommend it to other people?   Yes   No

Comments or suggestions (optional):

- -

Did Quiet Hour help you feel less tense or stressed?   Yes   No   Date: _____

Did it help you feel more calm or relaxed?   Yes   No

Would you recommend it to other people?   Yes   No

Comments or suggestions (optional):

- -

Did Quiet Hour help you feel less tense or stressed?   Yes   No   Date: _____

Did it help you feel more calm or relaxed?   Yes   No

Would you recommend it to other people?   Yes   No

Comments or suggestions (optional):

PARTICIPANT GIFT

If you'd like to offer parting gifts for participants, feel free to use the following Individual Guidance Summary Cards. Print or photocopy this page on cardstock as many times as needed, cut out the cards, and offer them at the end of each session for participants to take.

QUIET HOUR GUIDANCE

Step	~Minutes for 1 hr.	~Minutes for ½ hr.
Agreements	0	0
Get Comfortable	5	3
Gather	5	3
Breathe	5	3
Notice—Feeling	5	3
Notice—Seeing	5	3
Notice—Hearing	5	3
Notice—Smelling	5	3
Notice—It All	20	6
Appreciate	5	3

QuietHour.org

QUIET HOUR GUIDANCE

Step	~Minutes for 1 hr.	~Minutes for ½ hr.
Agreements	0	0
Get Comfortable	5	3
Gather	5	3
Breathe	5	3
Notice—Feeling	5	3
Notice—Seeing	5	3
Notice—Hearing	5	3
Notice—Smelling	5	3
Notice—It All	20	6
Appreciate	5	3

QuietHour.org

QUIET HOUR GUIDANCE

Step	~Minutes for 1 hr.	~Minutes for ½ hr.
Agreements	0	0
Get Comfortable	5	3
Gather	5	3
Breathe	5	3
Notice—Feeling	5	3
Notice—Seeing	5	3
Notice—Hearing	5	3
Notice—Smelling	5	3
Notice—It All	20	6
Appreciate	5	3

QuietHour.org

QUIET HOUR GUIDANCE

Step	~Minutes for 1 hr.	~Minutes for ½ hr.
Agreements	0	0
Get Comfortable	5	3
Gather	5	3
Breathe	5	3
Notice—Feeling	5	3
Notice—Seeing	5	3
Notice—Hearing	5	3
Notice—Smelling	5	3
Notice—It All	20	6
Appreciate	5	3

QuietHour.org

QUIET HOUR
GUIDANCE FOR GROUP LEADERS SUMMARY

Once you are familiar with the Quiet Hour process, feel free to print or photocopy this shorter version and laminate it to use often. Then use its prompts as reminders of the steps in the full narration and say them fully in your own words.

Step	Approx. Minutes	Running Total
[INTRODUCTION] Welcome, Interpretation? Benefits of this	4	4
[AGREEMENTS] Detach from devices, maintain quiet, Questions?	4	8
[GET COMFORTABLE] Find spot nearby, maybe take off shoes	4	12
[GATHER] Bring your thoughts and energy to here and now	4	16
[BREATHE] Maybe extend exhale, in 1, 2, 3, out 1, 2, 3, 4	4	20
[NOTICE—FEELING] The surface supporting you, sunlight, air	4	24
[NOTICE—SEEING] At eye-level, above, below, near, far	4	28
[NOTICE—HEARING] Main sounds, quieter sounds, near, far	4	32
[NOTICE—SMELLING] Overall scent, individual natural things	4	36
[NOTICE—IT ALL] For a longer time, relax, just be	10	46
[APPRECIATE] Something here, it all, yourself for doing this	4	50
[CONCLUSION] Can use this in daily life in other times and spots	4	54
[SURVEY & GIFT] [OPTIONAL]	6	60

Handling Potential Challenges

[HUMAN-MADE NOISE] Relax resistance, shift focus, humans are part of nature, too

[WEATHER] Relax resistance, shift focus to something positive about it

[RESTLESSNESS] Stretch, face different direction, extended exhale breathing

[DISRUPTIVENESS] Take aside, ask if need anything, remind of agreements

QuietHour.org

QUIET HALF-HOUR
GUIDANCE FOR GROUP LEADERS SUMMARY

Once you are familiar with the Quiet Hour process, feel free to print or photocopy this shorter version and laminate it to use often. Then use its prompts as reminders of the steps in the full narration and say them fully in your own words.

Step	Approx. Minutes	~Running Total
[INTRODUCTION] Welcome, Interpretation? Benefits of this	2	2
[AGREEMENTS] Detach from devices, maintain quiet, Questions?	2	4
[GET COMFORTABLE] Find spot nearby, maybe take off shoes	2	6
[GATHER] Bring your thoughts and energy to here and now	2	8
[BREATHE] Maybe extend exhale, in 1, 2, 3, out 1, 2, 3, 4	2	10
[NOTICE—FEELING] The surface supporting you, sunlight, air	2	12
[NOTICE—SEEING] At eye-level, above, below, near, far	2	14
[NOTICE—HEARING] Main sounds, quieter sounds, near, far	2	16
[NOTICE—SMELLING] Overall scent, individual natural things	2	18
[NOTICE—IT ALL] For a longer time, relax, just be	5	23
[APPRECIATE] Something here, it all, yourself for doing this	2	25
[CONCLUSION] Can use this in daily life in other times and spots	2	27
[SURVEY & GIFT] *[OPTIONAL]*	3	30

Handling Potential Challenges

[HUMAN-MADE NOISE] Relax resistance, shift focus, humans are part of nature, too

[WEATHER] Relax resistance, shift focus to something positive about it

[RESTLESSNESS] Stretch, face different direction, extended exhale breathing

[DISRUPTIVENESS] Take aside, ask if need anything, remind of agreements

QuietHour.org

GROUP LEADER SURVEY

If you are testing the program, after the test period, feel free to print or photocopy this survey, complete it, and have other leaders who led Quiet Hour sessions complete it.

Was leading Quiet Hour easy?   Yes   No   Date: _____

Do you think it helped participants?   Yes   No

Would you recommend it to other program leaders? Yes   No

Comments or suggestions (optional):

ANNOUNCEMENT AND FLYER

For your convenience, here are two ways to spread the word about your event(s): a brief announcement and a flyer. If you are hosting Quiet Half-Hour, adjust the wording, age range, and timeframe accordingly.

Brief Announcement

Below is the brief announcement. Add the day, date, time, and location of your event(s). Then post it on your social media channels, submit it for inclusion in calendars of events, etc. Also, you are welcome to expand the wording into a longer press release and send it to local media outlets.

QUIET HOUR

Enjoy a break from noise and busy-ness. Experience a peaceful, 4-step process to help you de-stress and relax in nature. This seated program is for all abilities, ages 12 and older.

[DAY, DATE, START TIME, END TIME, LOCATION]

Flyer

To further raise awareness of your event(s), on the following page you will find a template for a flyer.

To use it, first print or photocopy the page to make as many copies as you need. Second, on the copies, write in the day, date, time, location, and contact information for your specific event(s). Then lastly, you can post your customized flyers on bulletin boards and/or have stacks of them available for people to take at other events before your event(s).

If your organization has any kind of newsletter, feel free to send one of your customized flyers to the editor, so they can feature it in an issue of the newsletter before your event(s).

Although the title of the flyer is "Quiet Hour," you can also customize it for Quiet Half-Hour. To do that, just draw a chevron before "Hour" and, near it, write "Half-." Your start and end times will also indicate the session is a half-hour.

Quiet Hour

An Easy Way to Feel Inner Peace Outside

Enjoy a break from noise and busy-ness. Experience a peaceful, 4-step process to help you de-stress and relax in nature. This seated program is for all abilities, ages 12 and older.

Day: _____ Date: _____

From: _____ To: _____

Place: _____

Contact: _____

RESOURCES

"I go to nature to be soothed and healed,
and to have my senses put in order."

—John Burroughs

WEBSITES AND BOOKS

Natural Space Locators

The following online tools can help you find natural spaces (mostly in the U.S.) to do Quiet Hour. If you are in another country, an online search might help you find similar tools for that country.

- AllTrails.com

- DiscoverTheForest.org

- ParkServe.tpl.org/mapping/index.html

- QuietParks.org/quiet-places

- TrailLink.com

Related Books

Li, Qing. *Into the Forest: How Trees Can Help You Find Health and Happiness*, UK: Penguin Random House UK, 2019.

Louv, Richard. *Last Child in the Woods: Saving Our Children from Nature-deficit Disorder*, North Carolina: Algonquin Books, 2008.

Williams, Florence. *The Nature Fix: Why Nature Makes Us Happier, Healthier, and More Creative*, New York: W. W. Norton & Company, 2017.

Zorn, Justin and Marz, Leigh. *Golden: The Power of Silence in a World of Noise*, New York: Harper Wave, 2022.

ABOUT THE AUTHORS

Heather Chase and Ken Beller, a married couple, drew on their experience of nature's calming effect, plus decades of practice and study in personal growth and stress reduction techniques, to create Quiet Hour.

They are coauthors of the book *Great Peacemakers*, winner of 30+ awards and endorsed by 3 presidents and 3 Nobel Peace Prize winners. They also create popular online courses as well as workshops and keynote speeches for many non-profit organizations and Fortune 500 companies.

They live in the American Southwest. They welcome feedback and can be reached at GreatPeacemakers.com and QuietHour.org.

Made in the USA
Coppell, TX
08 December 2022

88132260R00026